Music Minus One
VOCALS

10 SELECTIONS FROM THE HIT MUSICAL
WITH SOUND-ALIKE BACKING TRACKS ONLINE

H★MILTON

AN AMERICAN MUSICAL BY LIN-MANUEL MIRANDA

T0081620

PLAYBACK+
Speed • Pitch • Balance • Loop

To access audio visit:
www.halleonard.com/mylibrary

"Enter Code"
2432-8967-4518-6243

ISBN 978-1-4950-7133-1

WARNER CHAPPELL MUSIC

EXCLUSIVELY DISTRIBUTED BY

HAL•LEONARD®

Visit Hal Leonard Online at
www.halleonard.com

Contact us:
Hal Leonard
7777 West Bluemound Road
Milwaukee, WI 53213
Email: info@halleonard.com

In Europe, contact:
Hal Leonard Europe Limited
42 Wigmore Street
Marylebone, London, W1U 2RN
Email: info@halleonardeurope.com

In Australia, contact:
Hal Leonard Australia Pty. Ltd.
4 Lentara Court
Cheltenham, Victoria, 3192 Australia
Email: info@halleonard.com.au

Alexander Hamilton

Words and Music by Lin-Manuel Miranda

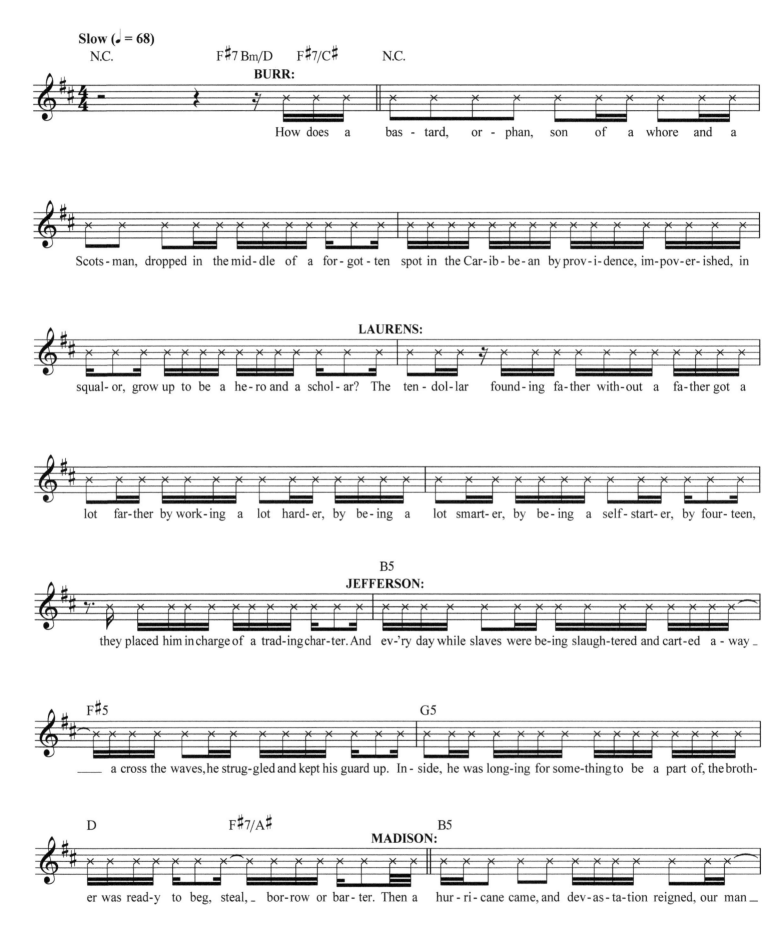

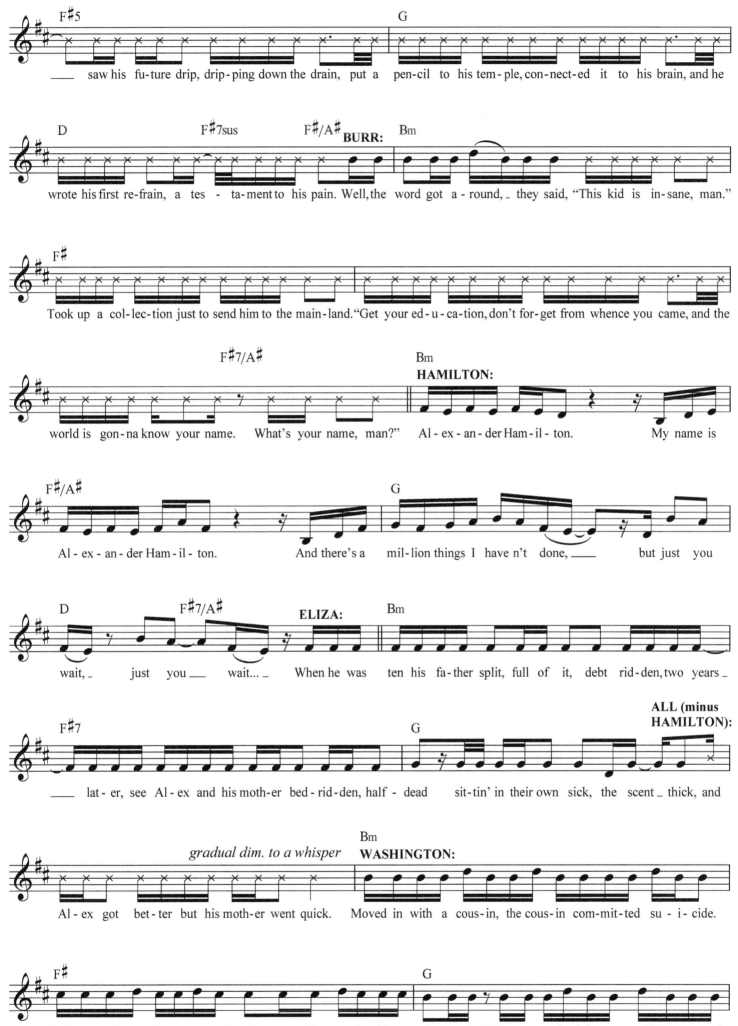

saw his fu-ture drip, drip-ping down the drain, put a pen-cil to his tem-ple, con-nect-ed it to his brain, and he

BURR:

wrote his first re-frain, a tes - ta-ment to his pain. Well, the word got a - round, they said, "This kid is in-sane, man."

Took up a col-lec-tion just to send him to the main-land. "Get your ed-u-ca-tion, don't for-get from whence you came, and the

HAMILTON:

world is gon-na know your name. What's your name, man?" Al - ex - an - der Ham-il - ton. My name is

Al - ex - an - der Ham-il - ton. And there's a mil-lion things I have n't done, but just you

ELIZA:

wait, just you wait... When he was ten his fa-ther split, full of it, debt rid-den, two years

ALL (minus HAMILTON):

lat - er, see Al - ex and his moth-er bed - rid-den, half - dead sit-tin' in their own sick, the scent thick, and

gradual dim. to a whisper **WASHINGTON:**

Al - ex got bet - ter but his moth-er went quick. Moved in with a cous-in, the cous-in com-mit-ted su - i- cide.

Left him with noth-in' but ru-ined pride, some-thing new in-side, a voice say-in', "You got-ta fend for your-self." He start-ed

My Shot

Words and Music by Lin-Manuel Miranda
with Albert Johnson, Kejuan Waliek Muchita, Osten Harvey, Jr., Roger Troutman, Christopher Wallace

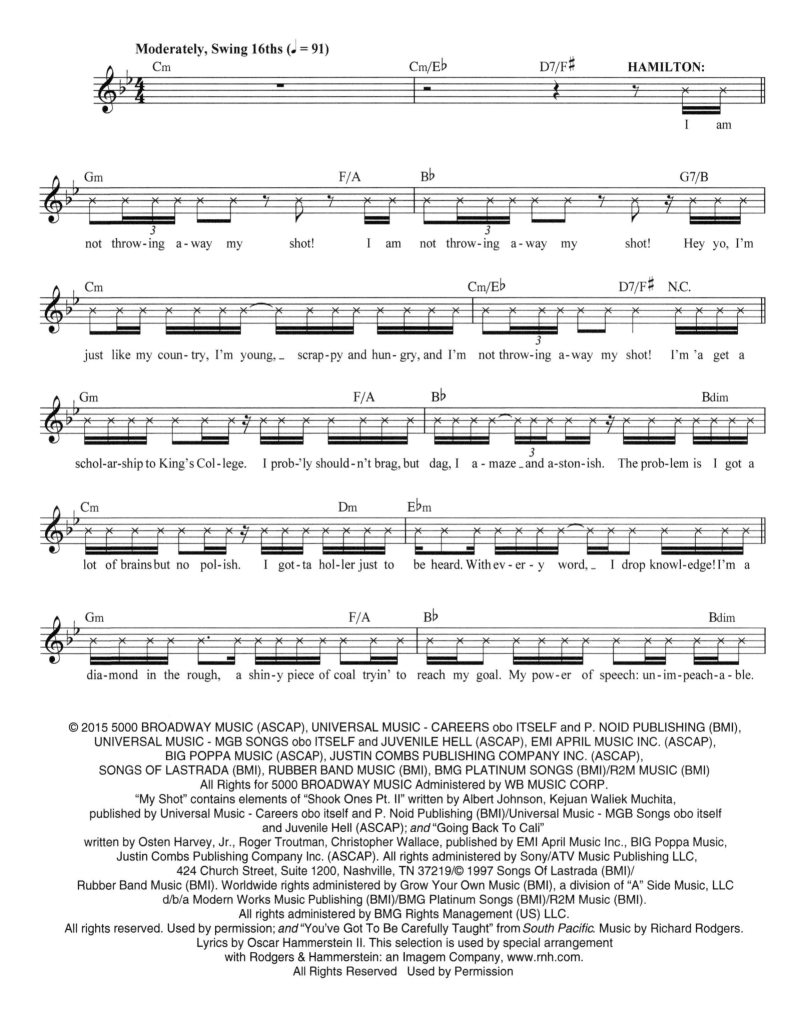

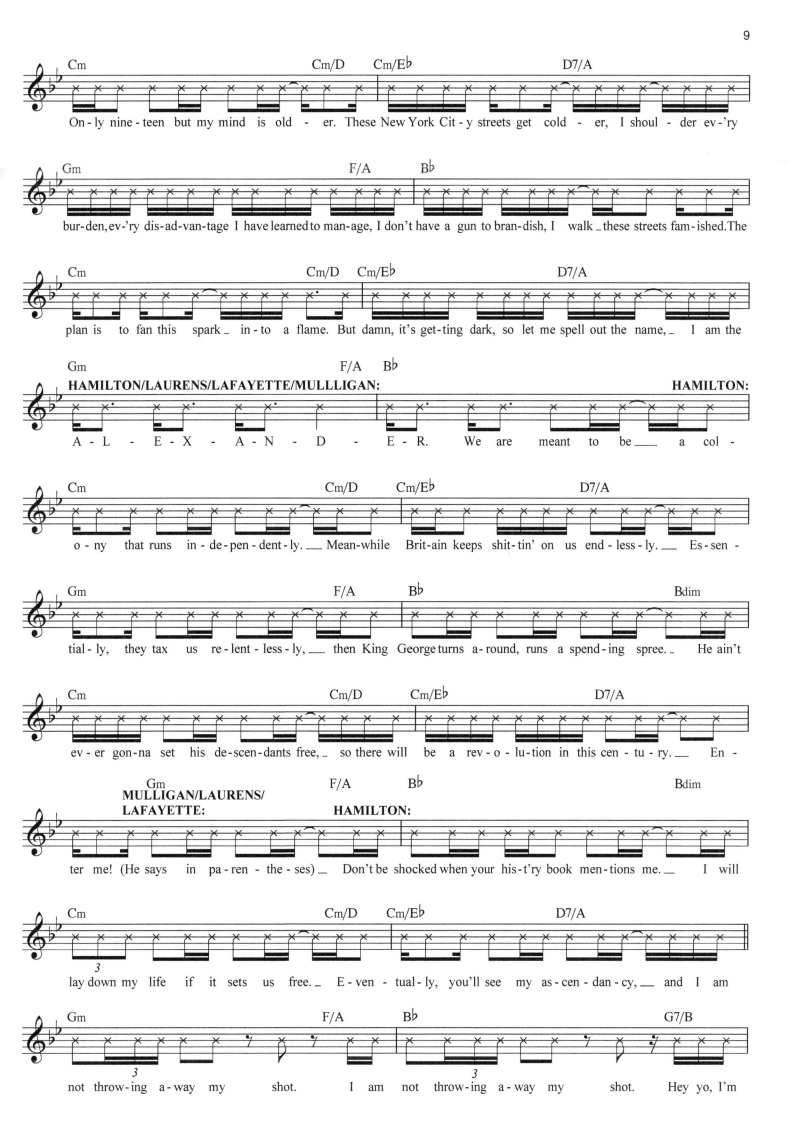

Cm   Cm/D   Cm/E♭   D7/F♯   G7/B

just like my coun-try, I'm young, _ scrap-py and hun-gry, and I'm not throw-ing a-way my shot. I am

Gm   F/A   B♭

HAMILTON/LAURENS:

not throw-ing a-way my shot. I am not throw-ing a-way my shot. Hey yo, I'm

Cm   Cm/D   Cm/E♭   D7/F♯

just like my coun-try, I'm young, _ scrap-py and hun-gry, and I'm not throw-ing a-way my shot. It's time to

Gm   N.C.

LAFAYETTE:

take a shot! I dream of life with-out a mon-ar-chy. The un - rest in France _ will lead to 'on - ar - chy?

'On - ar - chy? How you say, how you say, "an - ar - chy?" When I fight, I make the oth - er side pan-ick - y with

Gm   N.C.

MULLIGAN:

my shot! Yo, I'm a tail-or's ap-pren - tice, and I got y'all knu-ckle-heads *in lo - co par-en - tis.* I'm

join-ing the re-bel-lion _'cause I know it's my chance _ to so-cial - ly ad-vance, _ in-stead of sew-in' some pants! _ I'm gon-na

Gm   N.C.

LAURENS:

take a shot! But we'll nev-er be tru-ly free un - til those in bon-dage have the same rights as you and me, you

and I. Do or die. Wait till I sal-ly in on a stal-li-on with the first black bat-tal - i - on. Have an-

Gm   **BURR:**   F/A   B♭   G7/B

oth - er shot! Gen-ius - es, low - er your voic - es. You keep out of trou-ble and you dou-ble your choic - es. I'm

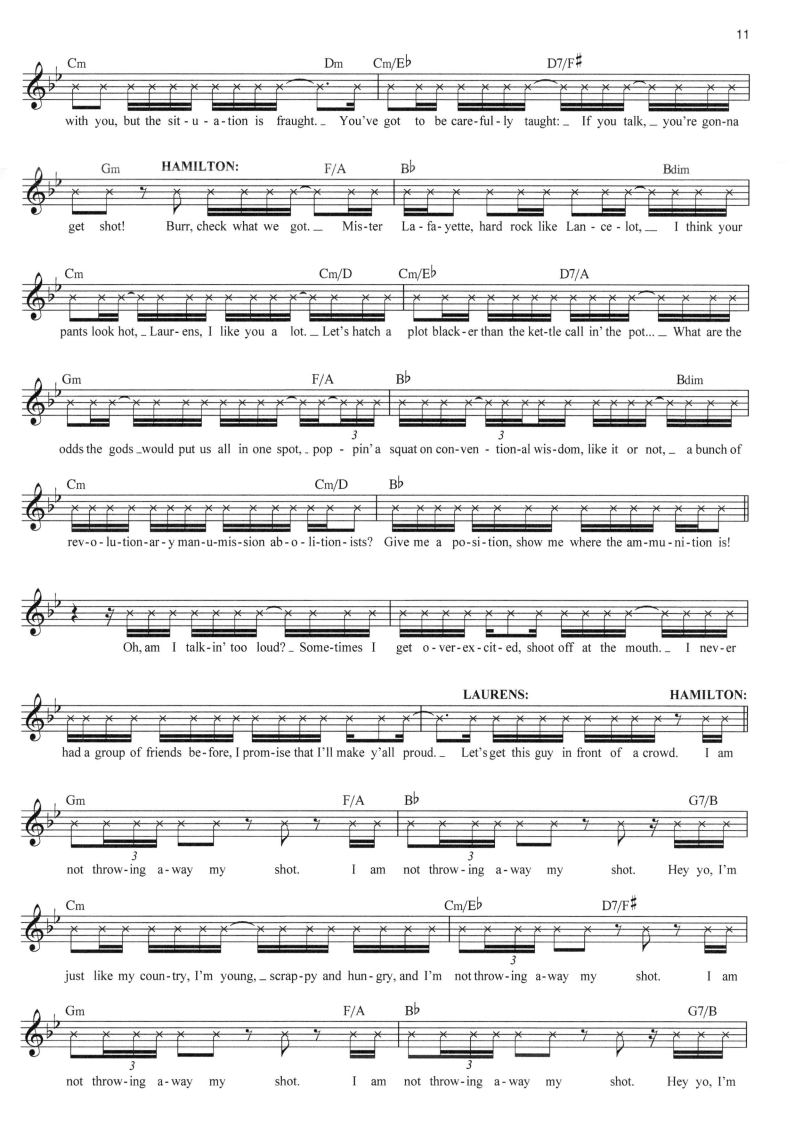

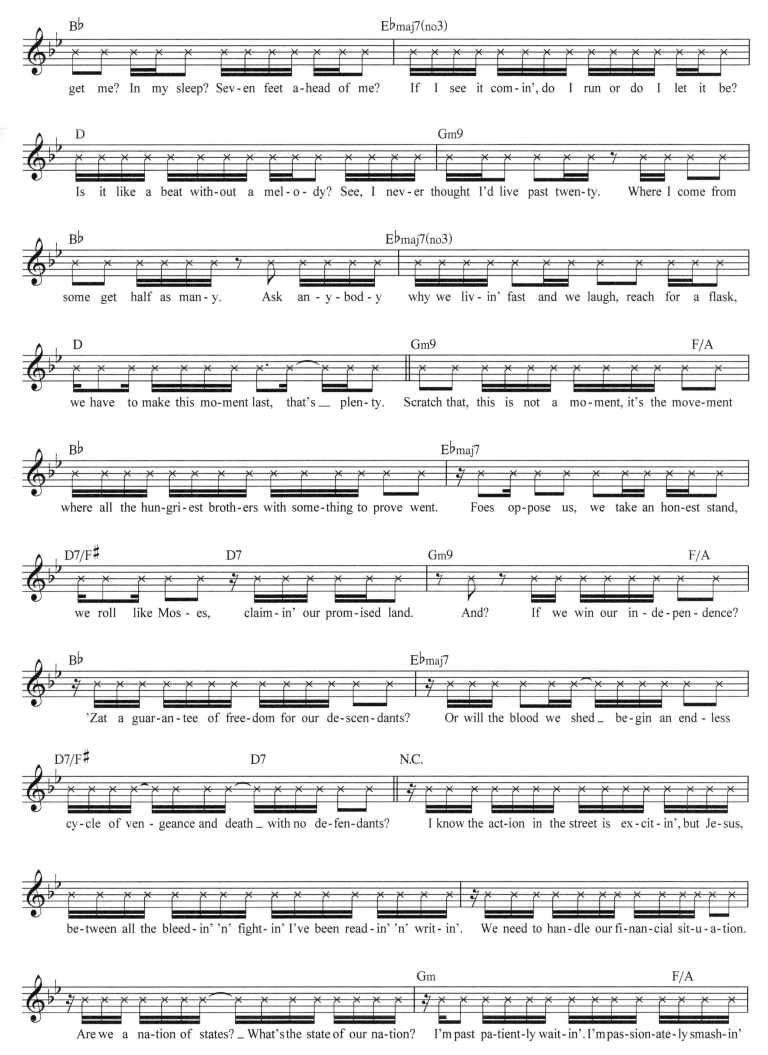

You'll Be Back

Words and Music by Lin-Manuel Miranda

Helpless

Words and Music by Lin-Manuel Miranda

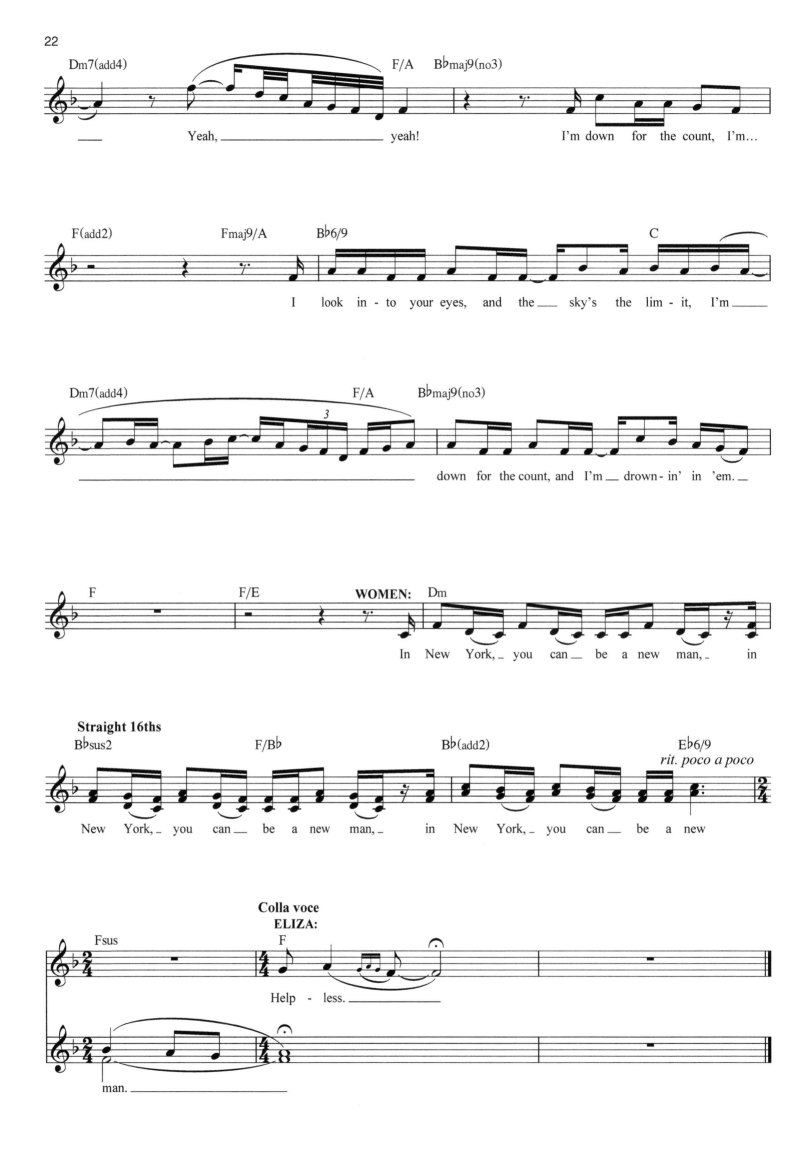

Wait for It

Words and Music by Lin-Manuel Miranda

That Would Be Enough

Words and Music by Lin-Manuel Miranda

Dear Theodosia

Words and Music by Lin-Manuel Miranda

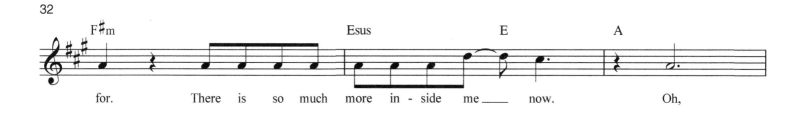

F#m　　　　　　　　　　Esus　　　E　　　A

for.　There is　so　much　more　in - side　me ____ now.　　Oh,

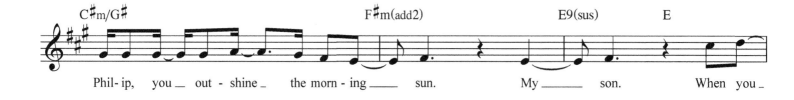

C#m/G#　　　　　　　　　　　F#m(add2)　　E9(sus)　　E

Phil- ip,　you ___ out - shine ___ the morn - ing ____ sun.　My ____ son.　When you ___

A　　　　C#m7/G#　　　　　F#m(add2)　　　　Esus　E

____ smile,　　I fall a - part. ___　And I thought I　was ___ so ___ smart.

D　　　E　　D　　　　E　　D　　　　E

BURR:

My　fa - ther was - n't　a - round. _　　I'll be a - round ___

HAMILTON:

My　fa - ther was - n't　a - round. _　　I swear that I'll be a - round ___

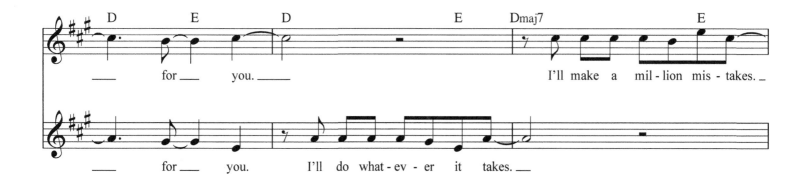

D　　　E　　　D　　　　　E　Dmaj7　　　　　E

____ for ___ you. ____　　I'll make a　mil - lion mis - takes. ___

____ for ___ you.　I'll do what - ev - er　it　takes. ___

What'd I Miss

Words and Music by Lin-Manuel Miranda

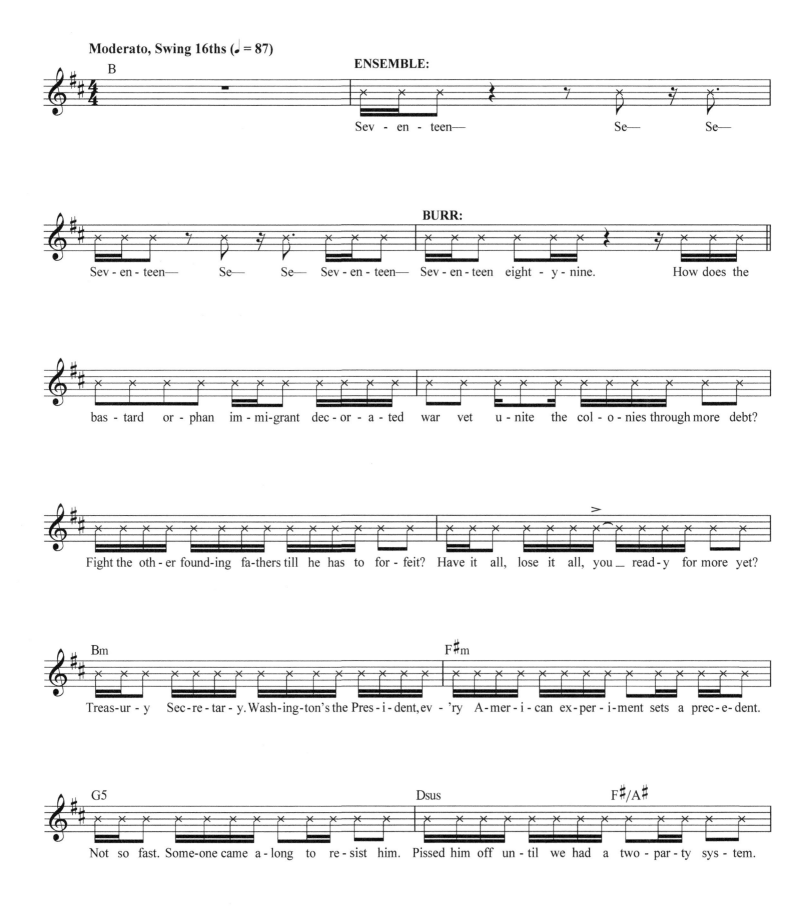

world still __ spins. __   I helped La - fay - ette __ draft a dec - la - ra -

- tion, then I said, __ "I got - ta go. __   Got - ta be in Mon - ti - cel -

- lo."   Now the work at home __ be - gins...   Aaa - ooo!   So what -'d I __

Double-time, Swing-era Jazz (♩ = 178)

__ miss?   What -'d I _____ miss?   Vir -

gin - ia, my home __ sweet home, __ I wan - na give you a kiss. __

I've been in Par - is meet - ing lots of dif - f'rent la - dies.   I guess I

ba - sic - 'lly missed __ the late eight - ies.   I trav - eled the wide wide __ world __

__ and came back to this... __   Aaa - ooo! There's a let - ter on my

Washington on Your Side

Words and Music by Lin-Manuel Miranda

Oh!

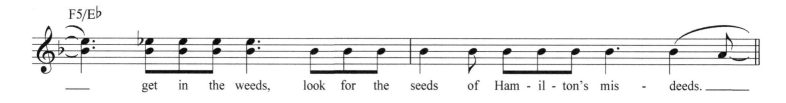

If we fol - low the mon - ey and see where it leads

get in the weeds, look for the seeds of Ham - il - ton's mis - deeds.

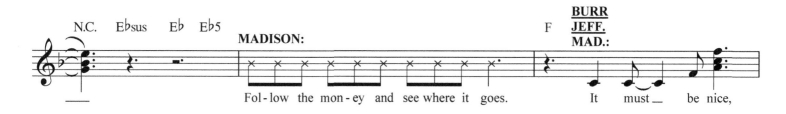

It must __ be nice, it must __ be nice. __

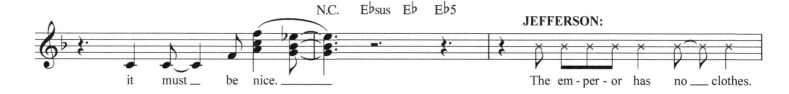

Fol - low the mon - ey and see where it goes. It must __ be nice,

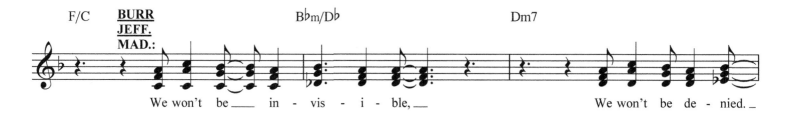

it must __ be nice. __ The em - per - or has no __ clothes.

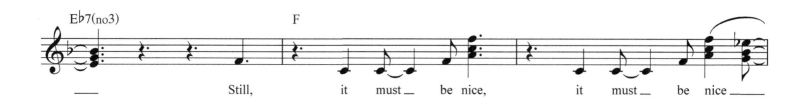

We won't be __ in - vis - i - ble, __ We won't be de - nied. __

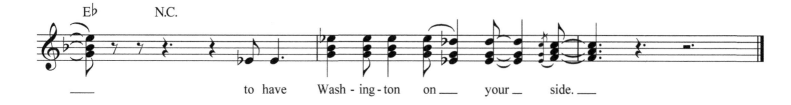

Still, it must __ be nice, it must __ be nice __ to have Wash - ing - ton on __ your __ side. __

Burn

Words and Music by Lin-Manuel Miranda

Moderate 2, icy (♩. = 66)

N.C.

ELIZA: *(2nd x only)*

keep vocal rhythms
conversational throughout

saved ev - 'ry let - ter you wrote me. ___ From the mo - ment I read them I knew you were

mine. You said you were mine. I thought you were ___ mine. ___

Bm — **F#** — **Gmaj7** — **D(add4)** **Em7**

Do you know what An - gel - i - ca said ___ when we saw your first let - ter ar - rive? She said,

Bm — **F#** — **Gmaj7** — **D(add4)** **D(add4)/C#**

"Be care - ful with that ___ one, love. He will do ___ what it takes to sur - vive." You and your

Bm — **F#** — **Gmaj7** — **D(add4)** **Em11**

words flood - ed my sens - es. Your sen - tenc - es left me de - fense - less. You built me

Bm — **F#** — **Gmaj7** — **D(add4)** **D(add4)/C#**

pal - ac - es ___ out of par - a - graphs, you built ca - the - drals. ___ I'm re -

Bm — **F#/A#** — **Gmaj7** — **D** **Em7**

read - ing the let - ters you wrote me. ___ I'm search - ing and scan - ning for an - swers in ev - er - y